Circular Knitting Machine Patterns for Beginners

The Ultimate Design Patterns and Projects for Newbies

Julie Jing

Table of Content

Introduction

Knitting is a technique for producing fabrics from yarn or thread. It is the method of creating fabric by transforming continuous strands of yarn into a series of interloping loops, each row of such loops hanging from the one immediately preceding it. The basic element of a knit fabric structure is the loop intermeshed with the loops adjacent to it on both sides and above and below it. Knitted fabrics are divided into two main groups: weft and warp knitted fabrics. Weft-knitted fabrics can be produced in circular or flat knitting machines.

The primary knitting elements are needle, cam, and sinker. With the variation of the elements, different characteristics of fabrics can be produced. The rising demands for knitted garments worldwide motivate researchers to research the various knitted fabrics and their production processes and develop new structures. Knitting machines comprise a needle holder that supports a plurality of needles, arranged side by side, and can be actuated with an alternating motion along their axis to the needle holder to form knitting.

In the circular knitting machine with many needles, the distance between the needles or sinkers has to be shrunk when the number of needles increases. This investigation is done to scrutinize the consequences of changing the knitting machine gauge. Gauge is a very important factor in a circular knitting machine, which denotes the density of the needles in the cylinder or dial.

This guide explicitly explores the different projects that could be performed in a circular knitting machine in a very simple and explanatory manner.

Chapter One

Knitting Machine Scrunchies

We will explore how to make knitting machine scrunchies. It is a super quick and easy project that can be made in 20 minutes from beginning to end, and it's a great way to use leftover yarn. The supplies are Loops and Thread impeccable yarn, a 48-needle Sentro knitting machine, a darning needle, and a hair elastic.

We will go through how to make three different-size scrunchies using two different seaming methods so you can see the differences in sizes and seams and choose which you prefer for your projects. The large scrunchies measure approximately five and a half by five and a half inches, the medium scrunchies measure about four and a half by four and a half inches, and the small scrunchies measure about three and a half by three and a half inches.

To begin, cast onto the knitting machine using a scrap yarn. Use a colour that contrasts well with the main colour to make seaming the scrunchie easier at the end.

To cast on, wrap your yarn around the first needle and then weave it back and forth around the needles until the end of the row when you see your first needle. When you see your first needle again, bring your yarn to the tension and choose the middle tension. Knit five rows in the scrap yarn.

Next, switch to the main color. You can cut a short tail on the scrap yarn but leave a very long tail in the main color because we'll need to use that tail to seam up the edge later. Knit 20 rows in the main color. Hold the two tails together close and low, and slowly begin cranking the machine, ensuring all the first few stitches are caught. Knit the first few rows slowly, and then you can pick up the speed after the first few rows. After knitting 20 rows, switch back to the scrap yarn for five rows.

Next, to cast off, cut a short tail on the scrap yarn and crank the machine a few rounds until the work falls off the needles. If the last few stitches get caught, remove them manually.

Pull your work out of the machine and gently stretch out the stitches. You'll end up with a short tube. Turn the work inside out so the bumpy stitches are on the outside and the V-shaped stitches are on the inside. Grab a hair elastic and make sure it has a good stretch. Scrunch your work together, no pun intended, and pull the elastic onto the work.

Next, look for whichever tail is longer, and use that tail to seam the sides of the scrunchie. We will explain how to seam the scrunchie with your darning needle, and on the next size, and how to seam it with a crochet hook. Line up the top loops of your main colour to match a bottom loop with the top loop, bring your darning needle through the bottom loop to under the top loop, and repeat the same process over and over until the end of the edge.

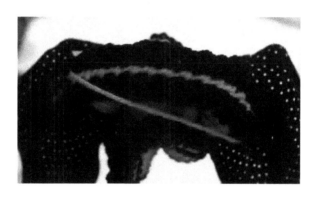

Make sure not to pull too tightly while you're seaming. When you get to the end, make sure you're catching the last couple of live stitches. Then, trim the tails to five or six inches and tie one quick temporary knot between the two tails. You don't need to tie the permanent knot now because we need to adjust the knot's tightness later. So, tie one quick knot to keep the tail secure.

Next, remove the scrap yarn. Generally, there'll be one side that pulls off easily and one side that's more of a challenge. For the side that's more of a challenge, identify the yarn looped through the top loop and use a crochet hook or a darning needle to pull it through. Once that yarn is pulled through the entire loop, the other loops will pull out much more easily.

Once you remove all your scrap yarn, double-check to ensure you don't miss any stitches. If you're all good and no live stitches are left, pull the knot between the two yarn tails tight and play with the tension to see what feels best for you. Secure the knot with a couple of tighter knots, and then use a darning needle to pull the tails into the middle of the work and trim the excess to weave in the ends. Use a knitting tag on the work. If you use a knitting tag, cover the knot where you knotted the tails together.

<u>Medium Size</u>

Next, we will go through the medium size with a crochet seam. Follow the same procedure as the large size we knit earlier, except we will knit 15 rows in the main colour. Cast off the 15-row scrunchie and crochet the side closed.

Like earlier, line the loops up directly above and below each other. Put your crochet hook under the bottom loop directly to the left of the yarn tail, then pull the top loop through. Next, pull the next loop on the bottom through and then the loop on the top. Continue in this process, alternating between the top and bottom loops until you finish the row.

Then follow the same process as before to secure your tails with knots, remove your scrap yarn, weave in your ends, and add your tag.

Small Size

Knit a small-size scrunchie, which will be 10 rows in the main colour, following all the same processes as the first two. The scrunchies are complete. Below is the large size, which is 20 rows. The medium size is 15 rows, and the small size is 10 rows. You can see the differences between the sewn and crocheted seams.

Chapter Two

How to Knit a Bow Headband

This section will explore knitting a bow headband using a circular knitting machine. We will go through how to make the small, medium, and large headbands and share how to knit an extra-large bow. Remember that tension varies from person to person and yarn to yarn, so knit up a sample headband to see how the sizing works. Depending on your yarn intention, You might need to make them smaller or larger.

There are so many ways to customize the headbands. You can make the bow smaller or larger, add an embellishment to the front of the bow, knit the bow in a different colour from the headband, or use a different colour for the centre of the bow.

All the sizes in this illustration measure approximately three inches tall. The small size measures about eight and a half inches wide, the medium measures about nine inches wide, and the large measures about nine and a half inches wide.

In terms of timing, this is a pretty quick project. It takes about 20 minutes to knit the pieces and about 10 minutes to seam and assemble the headbands, for about 30 minutes per headband. We all go at different paces, and the project time will vary from person to person.

The techniques in this project include casting on and off the knitting machine, seaming the ends, assembling the bow, using the mattress stitch, and adjusting the size of both the headband and the bow. We will use an Addi 22-needle machine for this project, or you can switch it out for the Sentro 22-needle machine. We will use Loops and Threads Impeccable yarn in Red Hot, Arbor Rose, and Soft Rose. You'll also need a crochet hook, a darning needle, a tape measure, and a knitting tag if you'd like to include one.

Step 1

Knitting the main piece of the headband. Cast onto a 22-needle machine using scrap yarn that you'll remove at the project's end. Wrap your yarn around the first needle and then weave the yarn front and back along the needles until the end of the row. When you reach your first needle again, place your yarn into the tensioner, hold the yarn in your hand to provide tension, and turn the knob to begin knitting.

Start slowly for the first couple of rows, and then you can slowly begin to pick up speed. Knit five rows in the scrap yarn. When you finish the five rows, cut the scrap yarn and throw it in the middle of the machine. Switch to your main color, leaving a long tail, which we'll use to seam the headband later.

Place the yarn tail next to the scrap yarn tail and hold it close and low as you slowly knit the next row. For the small size headband, knit 155 rows. For the medium size headband, knit 160 rows. For the large-size headband, knit 165 rows. And if you'd like to make the extra-large bow, knit 170 rows. In this illustration, we will be knitting the small size.

Remember that the headbands will stretch a bit over time, so when choosing your row count, you may err on the smaller side rather than the larger with your sizing.

When your work touches the table, bring it up inside the machine. If you're using a regular table, you'll need to do that a few times throughout knitting the piece, and after a while, you'll need to roll the work to keep it in the centre.

When you finish your main colour rows, cut a long tail in the main colour and throw it in the middle of the machine. Switch back to the scrap yarn and place the yarn tails together. Hold them close and low as you slowly knit the next row. Knit five rows in the scrap yarn.

When you finish five rows, cut a short tail on the scrap yarn and continue knitting until the work falls off the needles. Pull the work out of the machine, gently unroll the work, and stretch out the stitches. Put the work aside for now while we knit the next piece.

Step 2

Knitting the centre of the bow. Cast onto the same 22-needle machine again using scrap yarn in the same process as earlier. Knit five rows in the scrap yarn. Switch to your main colour yarn, leaving a long tail for all sizes. Knit 20 rows in the main colour yarn.

When you finish 20 rows, leave another long yarn tail and switch to the scrap yarn. Knit five rows in the scrap yarn. When you finish five rows, cut the yarn and continue knitting until the work falls off the needles. Pull the work out of the machine and gently stretch out the stitches. You'll now have two knitting pieces ready to assemble: the headband's main piece and the bow's centre.

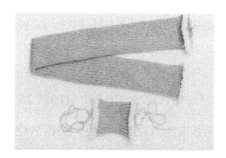

Step 3

Seaming the sides of the tubes. You'll notice that both pieces have open sides of the tubes. The next step is to use a crochet hook to seam the sides closed. Bring the sides of the tube together, lining up the stitches on top of each other with the two yarn tails to the left side. Ensure that when you arrange the stitches, there's one stitch to the right perpendicular to the rest.

Bring your crochet hook under that loop to the right and then pull through the stitch to its left on the top side. Pull through the stitch to its left on the bottom side. Continue in the pattern, pulling through the next stitch on the top, followed by the next stitch on the bottom until the end of the row.

Pull the yarn tail through when you reach the end of the row. Next, remove the scrap yarn by unwinding it around and around the work. Then, repeat the same process on the other side of the work and remove the scrap yarn. For the side that's more difficult to remove, identify the top length of yarn running through the stitches and remove the length a few stitches at a time until the end of the row. After removing the yarn, the rest should be removed much more easily.

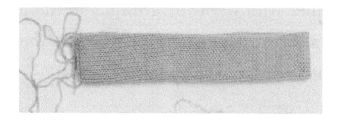

Next, repeat the same process on the sides of the smaller piece to seam the sides of the center of the bow and remove the scrap yarn from both sides.

We now have two finished and seamed pieces of knitting for the small size. The full length of the headband before assembling is 31 and a half inches. The medium and large sizes will be longer. The center of the bow might be a little less than 4 inches long.

Step 4

Assembling the headband. Lay the headband out horizontally. Fold one side in; the section should measure three and a half inches wide. Then, fold the other side in; the section should measure three and a half inches wide. Make the folded sections wider if you're making the extra-large size bow. Fold the bow sections as wide as needed to keep the headband size approximately eight to nine inches wide.

Alternatively, make the folded section smaller if you want a smaller bow. Remember that if you do a smaller bow, you'll need to knit fewer rows overall to avoid a headband that is too large. Then, pull both sides together. The bow section should measure seven inches wide when the headband is folded.

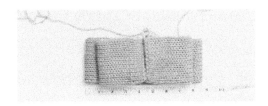

The headband should measure approximately eight and a half inches wide for the small size. When folded, below is how the headband will look at this point.

Next, seaming the bow to the headband. We'll be seaming the two sides of the exterior area of the bow to the layer below them and seaming the two headband sides together.

Step 5

Seaming the headband. Thread one of the long yarn tails onto a darning needle. Begin by threading through one side of the bow to the back of the bow. When you place your stitches on the back of the bow, ensure you're threading over the interior bars between the stitches to create a seamless look. Make sure you're not seaming horizontally over the V-shaped stitches.

Next, thread the needle through to the back of the bow, all the way to the back of the bow on the other side. Then, thread the needle back through to the top of the bow on the front. Repeat the same process, threading through the first side of the bow to the back, then threading the needle through to the back of the other side of the bow, and then back to the front. Continue in that process, pulling together all the sides until the end of the row.

As you work, make the stitches look clean on the back of the bow, but you don't need to worry too much about the stitches on top of the bow because we'll be covering that area with the centre of the bow later.

When you finish the row, you'll have yarn tails on both sides of the work. At that point, use a darning needle to bring both tails to the centre of the work, then tie both yarn tails securely with a few good knots and weave in the ends. When working with knitting machine tubes, it's easy to hide your ends; thread the yarn through a few inches into the work, trim the tail, and pull the work to bring the ends into the centre. Below is how your headband should look.

The bow sides should be attached, and the headband should be closed and wearable. At this point, remeasure and find that the headband is still about eight and a half inches wide, and the bow is about seven inches wide.

Step 6

Assembling the centre of the bow. To create the centre of the bow, use the mattress stitch to seam the sides to each other. Thread one yarn tail onto a darning needle and thread the needle through two interior bars on one side. Pull the yarn through, then thread the needle through two interior bars on the other side and pull the yarn through. Continue until the end of the row to create a small tube. Normally, we put much emphasis on creating a clean seam. However, for this piece, you don't need to worry about that particular seam looking perfect because it will end up on the inside of the work and won't be visible. So, just a quick seam will be fine. When you finish the row, tie the yarn tails together in a few good knots to secure the ends.

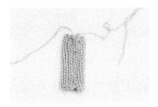

Step 7

Seaming the centre of the bow around the headband. Turn the headband inside out. Place the centre of the bow on the inside of the work with the seamed side facing towards the headband. Pull the sides together on the inside of the headband. Thread one of the yarn tails onto a darning needle.

To seam the sides together, thread the needle through both sides of one of the V-shaped stitches on the top and pull the yarn through. Then, thread the needle through both sides of one of the V-shaped stitches on the bottom side and pull the yarn through.

Pull the yarn fairly tightly as you work to create a secure seam. Continue in that pattern, alternating between top and bottom stitches until the end of the row.

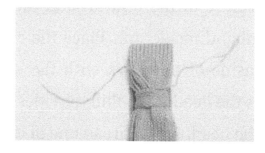

You'll now have two yarn tails. Secure the tails with a few good knots, and place the knot on the side of the centre, not on the top of the centre, to avoid the headband having a knot on the side that will rest against the person's forehead.

To weave in the ends, thread the yarn tails onto a darning needle and thread them horizontally across the centre of the bow, then turn around and go back the next row over. Do this about three times, and then trim the tail. Repeat the process with the second yarn tail. Turn the headband right side out.

Step 8

Adding a knitting tag. This part is optional; you can add a knitting tag to your work. For this pattern, use skinny knitting tags because the side area is pretty small when the headbands are folded flat, but a regular-size tag will also work fine.

If you prefer the bow to stay flat against the headband when worn, stitch it to keep it in place. Alternatively, you can keep it unattached. The bow headband is complete.

Chapter Three

How to Knit a Messenger Bag Purse

This section will explore knitting a small messenger bag using a circular knitting machine. We will make this pattern in three different sizes: the small size, which is a handbag; the medium size, which is a shoulder bag; and the large size, which is a crossbody bag. In this chapter, we will go through every step of the process.

The bag for this project measures approximately 8 inches wide. The small size measures about 11 inches tall, the medium measures about 18 inches tall, and the large measures about 22 inches tall. The bag is the perfect size to carry a phone, wallet, keys, and other small items.

There are so many ways to customize a bag. You can add a magnetic clasp, line the inside with fabric, add embellishments to the front, use double knitting to create a pattern on the outside, or try adding a pocket to the inside of the bag.

Regarding timing, it takes about one hour and 20 minutes from beginning to end to knit the small size, about 1 hour and 40 minutes to knit the medium size, and about 2 hours to knit the large size bag.

So, project time will vary from person to person. The technique in this section includes casting on and off a knitting machine, seaming the ends of a knitting machine tube, assembling a bag, and seaming pieces together using the mattress stitch. For this project, we will use a 46-needle Addi King Size Express knitting machine, but you can also make this with the Sentro 48-needle machine; your bag will be a touch wider.

We will Knit the bags using Loops and Threads of impeccable yarn in Putty, Aruba Blue, and Sea Green. We use less than one skein per bag for the small and medium sizes, and for the large size, we use a full skein plus about a quarter of a second skein. You'll also need stitch markers, a crochet hook, a darning needle, and a pair of scissors, as well as any solid item about two or three inches in height to help when we seam— a piece of cardboard— and if you'd like to include one, a knitting tag.

Step 1

Knitting the main piece. Begin by casting onto a 46- or 48-needle machine using scrap yarn. Wrap your yarn around the first needle and then weave the yarn back and forth along all the needles until the end of the row. When you reach the first needle again, thread the yarn into the tensioner. If you're using an Addi, hold the yarn in your hand to provide tension; if you're using a Sentro, place the yarn into the middle tensioner. Knit five rows in the scrap yarn.

When you finish five rows, cut a short tail on the scrap yarn and throw it into the middle of the machine. Then, leave a normal-length tail in the main colour yarn and throw it into the middle of the machine right next to the scrap yarn tail. Hold the two tails close and low as you slowly knit the next row. Go slowly at first, making sure it catches all of your stitches. Knit 110 rows in the main colour.

Leave an extra long tail in the main colours when knitting bags to use later when seaming. However, using a new yarn length for seaming is easier for this pattern than for the yarn tail. So, for the project, you can leave a normal-length yarn tail in the main colour.

A quick note about tension: tension can vary from person to person and from yarn to yarn. When you knit the project, your pieces might come out slightly shorter or longer. It is a forgiving project, so if your pieces come out longer or shorter, it's fine— your bag will just be a little taller or shorter. And in related news, if you'd like to knit a taller bag, knit more rows for the main piece. If you'd like to knit a shorter bag, knit fewer rows. Pull the work up inside the machine when your work touches the table.

When you finish 110 rows, switch back to the scrap yarn. Cut a normal-sized tail in the main colour and throw it in the middle of the machine. Then, cut a short tail on the scrap yarn and put it next to the main colour tail. Hold the two tails close together and low as you slowly knit the next row. Knit five rows in the scrap yarn.

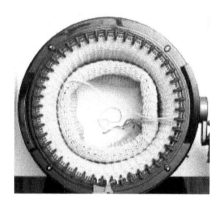

When you finish five rows, cut a short tail on the scrap yarn and continue knitting until the work falls off the needles. Pull the work out of the machine and gently stretch out the stitches. Put the work aside for now while we knit the handle.

Step 2

Knitting the handle. Switch to a 22-needle machine. Cast on like we cast on earlier, wrapping the yarn around the first needle and then weaving the yarn back and forth along all the needles until the end of the row. When you reach the first needle again, thread the yarn into the tensioner. Knit five rows in the scrap yarn. After five rows, please switch to the main colour and knit slowly to ensure it catches all your first few stitches.

For the small handbag, knit 130 rows; for the medium-sized shoulder bag, knit 200 rows; for the large-size crossbody bag, which is the bag we are currently knitting, knit 265 rows. Pull the work inside the machine when your work starts to touch the table. As you continue knitting, especially if you're knitting the large size, you'll need to roll the work as you keep it within the machine. It can get pretty tight at the end because the space inside the machine is so much smaller than the larger machine, but continue rolling the work, and then it'll fall as you knit further, repeat until the end of the project.

When you finish the number of rows needed for your handle, switch back to the scrap yarn. Knit five rows in the scrap yarn. When you finish five rows, cut a short tail in the yarn and continue knitting until the work falls off the needles. Pull the work out of the machine and gently stretch out the stitches. You should now have two finished pieces of knitting: the main piece of the bag and the handle.

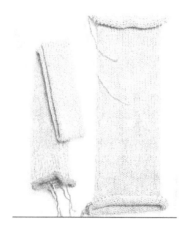

Step 3

Seaming the sides of the tubes. Both pieces have open sides of the tubes. The next step is to use a crochet hook to seam the sides closed. Bring the sides of the tube together, lining up the stitches on each other.

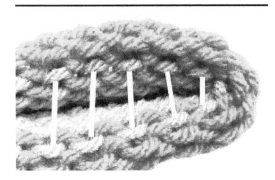

With the two yarn tails to the left side, ensure that when you arrange the stitches, there's one stitch to the right perpendicular to the rest.

Bring your crochet hook under the loop to the right and then pull through the stitch to its left on the top side. Pull through the stitch that's to its left on the bottom side. Continue in that pattern, pulling through the next stitch on the top, followed by the next stitch on the bottom until the end of the row. Pull the yarn tail through when you reach the end of the row; your side is now seamed.

Next, remove the scrap yarn. One side should be removed fairly easily; pull the yarn around and around until it pulls off completely, leaving just the seamed edge. Below is what the final seam will look like.

Next, turn the workaround and use the same process to seam the other side. For the side that's more difficult to remove, identify the top length of yarn running through the stitches and remove the length a few stitches at a time until the end of the row. After that yarn is removed, the rest should be pulled off much more easily.

Next, seam the sides of the handle. Follow the same process as earlier: use a crochet hook to seam both sides of the handle and remove the scrap yarn. Both pieces are now seamed, and the bag is ready to be assembled.

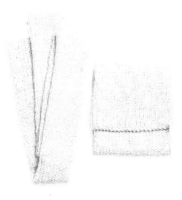

The main piece measures approximately 21 and a half inches long. The handle for the small size measures approximately 16 inches long, the handle for the medium size measures about 40 inches long, and the handle for the large size measures about 48 inches long.

Step 4

Assembling the bag. Lay your main piece vertically, fold the bottom third up, then the top third down.

Line up your handles on the side of the work, then open up the bag again and place any solid item about two to three inches tall in the middle. We will be using a roll of gaff tape, which works well, but you could use many items as long as they're a similar size. Bring the bottom of the bag back up over the item and work to align it evenly with the handles.

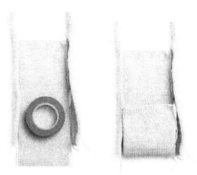

Step 5

Attaching the pieces with stitch markers. Use stitch markers to bring the work together where we'll be seaming. In some projects, you can get away without using the stitch markers even when they're recommended, but in this project, we suggest using them because they will help keep your piece seamed evenly. When you finish the stitch markers in the front, turn the bag around and add them to the corners. Then, turn the back over and add them to the back side, stopping at the same height as the front of the bag. As you use the stitch markers, placing them around the stitches directly under the bars you'll be using for the mattress stitch is helpful. The bottom half of the bag should measure about six inches tall, but the measurement will vary if you're knitting a shorter or longer bag. The bag is ready to seam.

Step 6

Seaming with the mattress stitch. If using the mattress stitch, the first step is identifying two rows of V-shaped stitches on either side of the pieces we'll be joining, going in the same direction. The images below are the rows to bring together the two pieces. Next, look for the bars inside the stitch directly next to the rows.

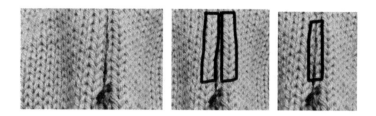

For the pattern, cut a new length of yarn for seaming. To assess how much yarn is needed, casually wrap the yarn around the entire length of what you are seaming, then double the length and usually add a little more to be safe. Then, thread the yarn onto a darning needle and secure it with a knot inside the purse's interior bar. Then, thread it through to the corner of the work.

Look for the bars we discussed earlier. Thread your needle through two bars on the other side of the work. Continue in that pattern, threading through two bars on one side and then two bars on the other until the end of the row.

As you near the stitch markers, remove them as you go. You can also go one stitch at a time if you prefer. Either one stitch at a time or two stitches at a time will work well for the front and back of the bag.

When you reach the corner of the bag, change the process a bit. For the sides, switch to alternating one stitch at a time. For the side with the handle, thread through the two bars of the bottom V-shaped stitch.

For the side of the main bag piece, continue threading through the same interior bars as we did earlier. Continue to the end of the row.

When you reach the corner, turn the work and return to the same mattress stitch style we used to seam the front of the bag.

As you near the end of the seam, make sure to check that you're ending the seam at the same height as the front of the bag. You might need to check that a few times as you work to ensure you're ending the back seam at the same height as the front piece.

When you've got it at the right place, pull through one more loop on the other side to keep the seam closed tightly. Thread the needle to the inside area a few stitches in, secure the yarn tail with a few good knots on an interior bar between the stitches, and then weave in the ends. Next, repeat the same process on the other side of the bag to finish attaching the handle.

Step 7

Weaving in and trimming the yarn tails. Your work will have lots of yarn tails left out. When working with knitting machine pieces, it's really easy to weave in the ends because there's a center area of the work where you can hide the yarn. Turn your bag inside out, secure all the yarn tails with knots, and then weave in and trim the tails. Turn the work back to the right side.

Step 8

Adding a knitting tag. This step is optional, so you can add a knitting tag to the work.

Step 9

Adding a little support. The bags are knitted items, so they have a little stretch. If you'd like to add a little support to the bottom, cut a piece of cardboard about the same size as the bottom and add it to the bag before putting in your items. Or, if you'd like more support, you can sew a fabric lining into the inside of the bag. The small messenger bag is complete.

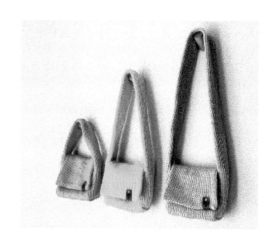

Chapter Four

DIY Knit Wristlet Purse

This section will explore how to knit a wristlet-style clutch purse using a circular knitting machine. It's a perfect size when you're on the run and need your phone, wallet, and keys in purse. It features a zipped closure, which keeps your items secure, and an i-cord knit wristlet, which makes it easy to carry.

We will go through the steps of the process in this chapter. The clutch measures approximately nine and a half inches wide by five and three-quarters inches tall.

The wristlet is approximately seven inches long. Regarding timing, it takes about 20 minutes to knit the purse, 20 minutes to knit the i-cord, and 30 minutes to seam the pieces and sew the zipper.

For the project, we will be using a 40-needle circular knitting machine, Loops, and Threads yarn in the color "lippy," a 9-inch pink zipper, a darning needle, a crochet hook, a pair of scissors, stitch markers, a sewing kit, and a knitting tag. We'll also use a pair of US size 9 double-pointed needles to hand-knit the i-cord, but if you prefer crochet, you can crochet the wristlet instead.

We'll begin by knitting the main piece of the bag. Cast onto a 40-needle circular knitting machine using scrap yarn. Wrap your yarn around the first needle and weave the yarn back and forth along the needles until the end of the row.

When you finish the row, place your yarn into the middle tensioner and remove the yarn at the end so the color doesn't matter; make sure it contrasts well with the main color, making it easier to seam at the end.

Knit five rows in the scrap yarn. When you finish the five rows, cut a tail on the scrap yarn and throw it in the middle of the machine. Then leave a long tail in the main color yarn, at least a few feet, because we'll need to use it later to seam up the bag and place it right next to the scrap yarn tail. Hold them close and low as you slowly knit your first row in the main color. For the purse, knit 100 rows in the main color.

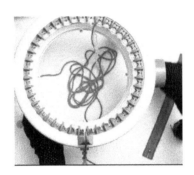

You can crank the machine by hand for the entire process. When you finish 100 rows, cut a long tail in the main colour and throw it in the middle of the machine. Then, switch back to the scrap yarn and knit five rows in the scrap yarn.

When you finish the five rows, cut a tail and crank the machine until your work falls off the needles. Pull the work off the machine and gently stretch out the stitches. Set aside the piece while we knit the i-cord.

For the purse, we can hand-knit the wristlet; however, this part is flexible. You can create your crochet version or order faux leather wristlets online if you prefer crochet. Knitting an i-cord is quick and easy, so we'll go through the process, and then you can choose how you want to style your wristlet.

Grab a pair of US9 double-pointed needles and cast on four stitches. Use the long-tail cast-on, but any cast-on will work. Knit all four stitches. Then, when you reach the end of the row, instead of turning the needle-like we normally do in knitting, push the stitches to the right side of the current needle and then start knitting from the beginning again using the working yarn coming from the left side of the back of the work.

Knit all four stitches again. When you finish up, repeat the same process, pushing the stitches to the right side of the needle. After a few rows, you'll see that your knitting forms a round cord.

Continue in that pattern until your cord measures approximately 13 inches long. That is pretty flexible;

it'll still work if it's shorter or longer. When your cord is done, bind off the stitches: knit two stitches and then pull the first stitch over the second. Knit another stitch and pull the previous stitch over the new one. Repeat that until you have one stitch left, and then pull the yarn tail through and secure it with a knot.

Thread the yarn onto a darning needle and weave it through a few bottom stitches to round out the bottom shape. Leave the yarn tails long; we'll use that later to attach the cord to the purse. Set aside the cord for now while we seam the purse.

For the seaming project, graft the open ends of the tube together. Grafting the sides together is a little more complicated than the typical way we sew most hats or headbands, but if you're new to grafting, you'll get the hang of it after a little practice, and it's such a useful skill because it creates a beautiful seamless join.

To graft the sides together, thread the bottom tail onto a darning needle, line up your stitches, and use the yarn tail to go down through the first stitch on the top and then up through the stitch to its left. Pull the yarn through.

Next, go down through the stitch on the bottom and then up through the stitch directly to its left. Pull the yarn through. This time, you need to thread the needle down through the stitch that you came up out of on the previous row, then go up through the stitch directly to the left. Next, go back to the bottom layer and thread the needle down through the stitch you previously came up through, then go up through the stitch directly to the left and pull your yarn through. The image below is for the front and back stitches. Continue in that pattern, alternating between top and bottom stitches until the end of the row.

It would help if you pulled the yarn tail to bring the stitches together as you're working, but not too tight. If you pull too tightly, the stitches on the other side will look too small. They'll look too loose if you don't pull them tightly enough. So, as you work, check to ensure your tension looks good.

When you start to round the corner, you can turn the work inside out to finish the seam. Below is how the inside of the first half of the seam looks.

Continue to the end of the row. When you reach the end, pick up the last couple of stitches and tie a quick knot with the two yarn tails.

Next, remove the scrap yarn. Unlike when you seam one side at a time, you'll need to unwind around the work as you remove the yarn. One side will likely pull off easily; for the side that's a bit more challenging, identify the length of yarn running through the top layer of stitches and begin to pull that length out a few stitches at a time. And once you remove that one length, the rest of the scrap yarn will pull off much more easily.

Once you've removed your scrap yarn, tie the two yarn tails with a few knots to secure the ends. Don't trim or weave them in yet; tuck them away on the inside for now. Loosen up the work a bit with your hands. The sides of the clutch are now seamed.

Grafting the stitches together creates a separate line of knit stitches, bringing together the work fairly seamlessly. If you have the seam in the middle of the work, rotate the work so that the seam is now on the edge.

The next step is to seam the bottom of the bag. Identify the two lines of v-shaped stitches that sit flat at the bottom edge. Line them up so they aren't twisted, and then use a few stitch markers to pull the work together. Use the mattress stitch to separate the two sides and see the bars to go through.

Look for the bars inside the v-shaped stitch on the bottom and top row. Alternate between the two stitches during the seam. Thread your long yarn tail onto a darning needle and begin sewing under one of the bars on the top right side, followed by one on the bottom right. Continue until you're on the flat part, then alternating, picking up one bar on the top, followed by one bar on the bottom, until the end of the row. As you're seaming, the work might want to twist a bit. Ensure you're watching the entire piece and double-check that you're picking up the correct bars. Having the stitch markers in place will help a lot with this.

Continue seaming the mattress stitch, pulling off the stitch markers as you get near them until the end of the row. When you reach the end, stitch through the last remaining hole and then thread the yarn into the inside of the bag. At that point, you can secure your yarn tails with a few solid knots and then use your darning needle to weave the ends into the inside of the work and trim the ends.

Check the inside of your bag and see which side has the cleaner-looking seam. If the inside looks better, turn the work inside out. If the outside looks better, leave it.

Next, add a knitting tag to the work. Normally, we should add the knitting tag as the final touch, but because we'll be sewing the zipper into the top of the bag, we must add the knitting tag to the work first. You can place your tag wherever you prefer or skip that part. Place it on the right side of the work with the beginning of the zipper, which will start on the left side. With the knitting tag attached, it's time to sew the zipper.

We will use a nine-inch zipper. Place your zipper on top of the bag and get a feel for where you want it to sew into the work. Use a few pins to keep the zipper in place while sewing. If you can, find a thread colour that matches the main colour of your work. But if it isn't perfectly matched, don't worry too much because you shouldn't see it too much from the outside.

Place the thread into a regular sewing needle and bring it through to create two layers of the thread. Tie a few knots at the bottom of the two threads. Begin by bringing the needle through from the part of the zipper hidden in the back. Then, push the needle through the zipper to the outside of the bag. Bring the needle under the first line of stitches. It's a little tough to see the small needle, so point to the line of stitches. Sew as closely as you can to the zipper area so there won't be any of the fabric showing when you close your purse.

When you reach your knitting tag, sew as closely as you can to the edge, weave the thread through only the zipper fabric behind the tag, and start again as close to the tag as possible. Continue sewing all the way around to the end of the row. When you start to turn the corner, unzip the zipper to sew the second half onto the other side of the bag. Continue sewing until the end of the zipper.

If you want to secure the zipper even more, you can sew another round around the bottom of the zipper fabric area, and you can also try using a back stitch while you're working, bringing the yarn back after each stitch. When you finish the zipper, secure the thread with a knot on the underside of the zipper fabric, and the clutch is almost complete.

The last step is to add the i-cord to the zipper. If your darning needle is too big to fit through the zipper, use the pointy part of the needle to push the yarn tail through to the other side, then use the needle to push the other yarn tail the other way through the zipper.

Next, firmly tie the two yarn tails together a few times to secure the knot. Then, you can stitch through the bottom area a few times to make the join look nice and round. When you're done, weave the yarn tail up through the i-cord and then trim the tail. The wristlet clutch purse is complete.

Chapter Five

How to Knit Fingerless Gloves

This section will demonstrate how to make a pair of warm, cosy fingerless gloves using a circular knitting machine. We will use Loops and Threads Impeccable yarn in sea green for this project. We will use the Sentro 48-needle knitting machine, which would work on any hat-size circular knitting machine.

To cast on, roll your machine until you find your last needle. Set your counter back to zero. Put a loop around the last needle using your scrap yarn, and then begin weaving the yarn behind and in front of each needle. As you rotate the knob to turn the loom, alternate every other needle behind in front until you get back to the original stitch where you began.

Next, secure your scrap yarn into the tensioner and choose the middle tension. Now you're ready to knit. Turn the knob and knit five rows in the scrap yarn.

Next, grab your main colour, pull a decently long tail (go with a couple of feet to be on the safe side), and throw it in the middle of the machine. Then, insert the yarn into the tensioner using the middle tension.

Hold the tails of the two yarns together, keeping them close together and low. Reset your counter back to zero. Go slowly with the first few stitches because that is a common place to drop stitches. Make sure the machine is catching all the stitches.

To knit the glove, knit 50 rows in your main colour. When you finish your 50 rows, cut a long tail from the main colour and put it in the machine's centre. Switch back to the scrap yarn to finish up the project. Hold the tails of the yarn close together and go slowly as you switch to the scrap yarn.

Knit five rows in the scrap yarn. When you finish up your five rows, cut the scrap yarn, leaving the tail in the middle, and turn your knob as if to knit a few rows. After a few rows, the work will fall off the needles. You might need to manually pull off the work from the last one or two needles. Once your work is off the machine, pull the work apart and stretch it out fully.

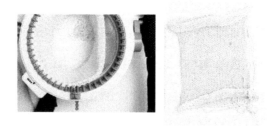

We'll be seaming the top and bottom of the tube. To do this, use a crochet hook and a darning needle. Hold your work and fold it together, leaving the two tails from the main colour and the scrap yarn out. Begin on the left side of the work, on the right-hand side.

First, identify the row you want to seam, which is the very top single row of the main colour. Start using your crochet hook to go through the first loop on the right side. Next, go through the next top loop and pull it through the first.

Do the same with the next bottom loop, crochet the next top loop, and then the next bottom loop. Continue in that manner to the end of the row. The seam is almost complete. Use your crochet hook to pull the tail through and tie a knot.

When the stitches are secured, pull out the scrap yarn. Usually, one side will be easy to do, and the other will be more challenging.

Next, flip to the other side of the work and do the same process on the other side. The glove is now fully seamed and ready to be sewn up. For reference, the glove unfolded should be nine and a half inches long and seven inches wide. It's about four inches wide, and the material is very stretchy when folded.

The fingerless gloves are assembled by sewing up the sides but skipping a couple of inches where your thumb will go. You can decide where to place the thumb hole depending on your hands or how high over the fingers you want the gloves to sit. For instance, start the thumb hole around 6 inches from the bottom of the glove. The thumb hole is about two inches long, leaving another two inches for the front of the glove.

Next, fold your glove in half and thread the long tail onto a darning needle. Use the mattress stitch to seam up the sides of the glove. The first step is to identify the row that you want to stitch. Locate the first two sets of V-shaped stitches. Pick up the bar between the stitches on the left side, and then pick up the same stitch on the right side of the work. Start by going through one stitch on the left-hand side, pulling the yarn through, then grabbing the corresponding stitch on the right side and pulling the yarn through again. Continue to make sure that your work is lined up properly. Continue the mattress stitch for 6 inches or until the area where you want to place your thumb hole.

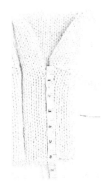

Once you reach 6 inches, begin thinking about starting your thumb hole. If the gloves are for yourself, this is a good time to try on the glove and see where you'd want your thumb hole to fit. Sew the yarn into only one glove side for about two inches. Look for the bar between the stitches and sew your yarn over and under the stitches for about two inches. When ready to begin sewing again, tie a quick knot to secure the opening. Continue in the mattress stitch until the end of the glove, then tie a few knots to ensure it's secure, and then weave in your ends.

Weaving in your ends in work created on a circular knitting machine is easy because you need to pull apart the tube a little, and you can hide the ends right on the inside. Next, you can add a knitting tag.

Chapter Six

How to Knit a Rainbow Hat

This section will demonstrate creating a cheerful rainbow hat using a circular knitting machine. This project will use Loops and Threads of Impeccable yarns in various rainbow colours. The Sento 48-needle knitting machine is our choice for illustration, but you can use any circular knitting machine suitable for hat sizes.

The first step is casting on with the beige. Find the white needle, then bring the beige behind and in front of each needle, encircling the loom.

When reaching the last stitch, place the beige into the tensioner, set it to medium tension, reset the counter to zero, and commence knitting. We're aiming for 64 rows in beige. After completing 64 rows, place your yarn skein in the machine's centre.

Next, knit two rows in red. Cut a tail around 8-10 inches in red, place it in the middle tensioner, and closely hold the yarn tails together as you start the next row, ensuring all stitches catch. After finishing the two rows of red, switch back to beige for another two rows.

Between rows, position your beige in the middle of the machine. Now, it's time for orange. Two rows in orange are up next. As you progress through colour changes, occasionally stop to tie temporary knots in the yarn tails. Secure the knots at the end when seaming up the hat so they don't need to be perfect.

Next, knit two more rows in beige. Knit two rows in yellow. Tie a few more temporary knots, and then back to beige for two additional rows. When your work touches the table, lift it within the machine to prevent tangling.

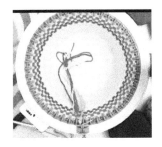

Next, add the two rows of green. Back to beige for two more rows, and now two rows in the blue. Back to beige for two rows, onto the last colour, two rows of purple. After the purple row is complete, knit 24 more rows in the beige. When you reach 110 rows, your hat is complete, and it's time to cast off.

Cut a long tail with your beige, at least a couple of feet, and use a darning needle to pick up every stitch around the machine. Next, remove the work from the machine and stretch it out.

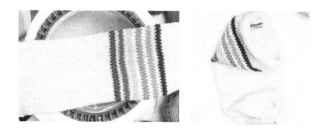

Before we assemble the hat, turn the tube inside out and finalize all the knots. Turn the work inside and out as you make the knots to tie it to the correct tension. When your knots are done, turn the tube right side out and use the tail at the bottom of the hat to cinch up the bottom. Next, tie a few knots to secure the bottom of the hat.

Afterwards, pull the bottom of your hat through to meet the top of the hat. Begin to cinch the top of the hat, leaving the tail from the bottom hanging on the outside. Tie a few knots with the yarn tail from the bottom and the yarn tail from the top to secure the bottom of the hat to the top.

Following that, weave in your ends. Weaving in the ends in a circular knitting machine tube is straightforward because you need to hide the yarn within the tube. Add a knitting tag to the items. Decide which pom-pom to use. Secure the pom-poms tight to the top of the hat so they sit nicely and close to the top.

Chapter Seven

How to Knit "Mommy and Me" Sized Hats

We'll go through the process of making adorable mommy and me hats on a circular knitting machine. We will use a Sentro 48 needle for this illustration, but feel free to use any circular knitting machine with a similar stitch count.

For the yarn, use Loops and Threads Impeccable yarn in light pink and beige, and use every inch of the beige, using one full skein and about half a skein of the pink.

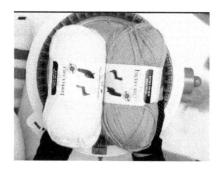

Start with the child-size hat. Begin by casting on 40 rows in the main colour. To cast on, look for the white needle. Use a decently long tail since the yarn is used to cinch the hat's top. Start by wrapping around the first needle and roll slowly, bringing the yarn behind one needle, then in front of the next, and so on – behind, in front. Continue this around the first row.

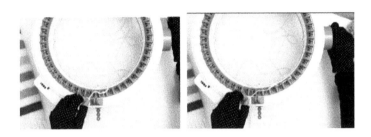

When you reach the end before the white needle where you put the loop on, bring it through and adjust the medium tension. Reset your counter to zero.

Now, we're set up and ready to go again. Knit for 40 rows, cutting the main colour when it passes the white needle. Please place it in the middle to the right side of the white needle. Grab your next colour, like the soft rose, leaving an 8-10 inch tail for safety. Perform 40 rows of the second color.

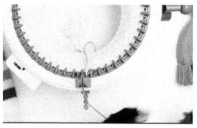 

Perform another 40 rows of the first colour, which, in this case, is white.

So, we have 40 rows of the main colour, 40 rows of the second colour, and 40 rows of the main colour. Next is to cast off by grabbing the stitches and pulling the needle. Continue like that all around the machine.

Next is to stretch out the work.

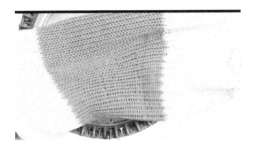

Prepare for Knots:

- Assemble the hat, ensuring knots are tied on the inside due to the use of two different colours.
- Turn the hat inside out to locate colour switches.
- Adjust knot tightness through trial and error by flipping it inside out.

Working in a Tube:

- Working in a tube eliminates the need to weave in ends; you can leave them as is.
- Optionally, make the ends shorter.
- Firm up the tube by turning it around.

Turning Right Side Out:

- After firming up, turn the hat right side out.

Tightening Ends:

- Two ends/tails will be visible.
- Choose the top and bottom sides; tighten the bottom with a needle and pull it in gently.
- Roll the hat inwards as it closes.
- Secure by tying a couple of knots with a darning needle.

Weaving in Ends:

- Cut yarns to a manageable size.
- Tie a couple of knots firmly without breaking the yarn.
- Weave in the ends; tube hats allow for hiding ends easily.

Choosing a Pom-Pom:

- Decide whether to fold up the brim, leave it as is, or add a pom-pom.
- Choose a pom-pom colour.

Attaching Pom-Pom:

- Thread the main colour yarn onto a darning needle.
- Go through the hat and come out on the top side, leaving a tail inside.
- Attach the pom-pom securely, going through its loop or structure.
- Reverse the process to secure the attachment.
- Flip the hat inside out and remove the needle.

Adding Tag:

- Add a tag to complete the hat.

Final Touch:

- The child-size hat is now complete.

Follow the same process for the adult size, with a slight modification. We'll do 50 rows of the main color, 40 rows of the brim, and another 50 rows of the main color. Follow the same steps as with the child size. The entire process only took a couple of hours using the mini machines.

Chapter Eight

DIY Knit Ballerina Doll

In this section, we will learn how to knit a ballerina doll using a circular knitting machine. We will go through every step of the process. The ballerina in this illustration measures approximately 11 inches tall by 3 inches wide. It can take about 20 minutes to knit the doll, 20 minutes to assemble, 25 minutes to add the facial and body features, and about 15 minutes to make the skirt, for approximately an hour and 20 minutes. We all go at different paces, making the project time vary from person to person.

SIZING:
11" TALL

The techniques we will use include casting on and off a knitting machine, assembling a knit doll, adding body and facial features, knitting a doll skirt, and hand-knitting a bow.

We will use an Addi 22 needle machine for this project, but you can also knit with the Sentro 22. We will use the Addie 46-needle Express King Size machine for the skirt, but you can switch that out for the Sentro 48. We will knit with Loops and Threads impeccable yarn in chocolate brown, soft rose, and soft taupe.

We'll also need stuffing, embroidery thread or black yarn, hair elastic, a crochet hook, a darning needle, and scissors. You can use a knitting tag, and if you'd like to hand-nit the bow, a pair of size seven US needles can be used, although you could easily swap that out for a crochet hook.

Step 1:

knit the doll. To knit the doll, start with the hair and work down to the feet. Then, reverse direction and work from the feet back to the hair.

Begin by casting onto a 22-needle machine using the hair color. Start with scrap yarn in many patterns, but we won't be using any scrap yarn for this project. Cast on directly with your first color, the hair color.

Wrap your yarn around the first needle and then weave the yarn back and forth along the needles until the end of the row. When you finish the row, place the yarn into the tensioner. Hold the yarn in your hand to provide tension. Turn the knob to begin knitting. Start slowly for the first couple of rows, and then you can start to pick up speed.

Knit 22 rows for the hair. When you finish 22 rows, cut a short tail around five or six inches in the hair colour and throw it in the middle of the machine.

Switch to the yarn you're using for the face. Put the two yarn tails between the same needles and hold them close and low as you slowly knit your next row, ensuring the first few stitches are caught. Knit 11 rows for the face.

After each colour change, after about four or five rows, tie a quick temporary knot between the two previous yarn tails. Please don't do a double knot because we'll come back at the end to finalize the knots. Just one quick knot is great.

When you finish 11 rows, switch to the yarn colour for the shirt. Knit 14 rows for the shirt. When you finish the shirt, switch to the yarn colour for the legs. Knit 12 rows for the legs.

When you finish the legs, switch to the colour for the ballet shoes. Knit 10 rows for the ballet shoes.

Next, work back up to the hair. Switch back to the yarn colour you're using for the legs. Knit 12 rows for the legs. When you finish the legs, switch to the yarn colour you used for the shirt. Knit 14 rows for the shirt.

When you finish the shirt, switch back to the yarn colour you used for the face. Knit 11 rows for the face. When you finish the face, switch back to the yarn colour you used for the hair. Pull the knitting up inside the machine when the work touches the table. Knit 22 rows in the hair. We're done knitting the body of the doll.

Next, cast off the stitches. Cut a long tail in the hair colour and thread the tail onto a darning needle. Turn the knob to move a few stitches to the right. Identify the stitch from which the yarn tail is coming out. Begin picking up stitches with the needle directly to the left of that needle.

Pick up the stitches one at a time for the first few stitches. After a few, pick two or three stitches at a time. Continue until the last stitch, turning the knob every few rows to advance the next stitches. Pick up the last stitch and then pull the work off the machine.

Gently stretch out the stitches. Put aside the work for now, and return to seam and assemble the doll l

Step 2:

knitting the skirt. Switch to a 46 or 48-needle machine for the skirt. Use scrap yarn to cast on. Remove the yarn at the end of the project, so the colour doesn't matter as long as it contrasts well with the skirt colour. Cast the same way as earlier, wrapping your yarn around the first needle and then weaving it back and forth along all the needles until the end of the row.

When you reach your needle again, put your yarn into the tensioner and hold it with your hand to provide tension as you begin to knit. Knit five rows in the scrap yarn. When you finish the five rows, leave a long tail in the skirt colour and place the tail next to the scrap yarn tail between the same needles.

Hold the two tails close and low as you slowly knit your next row. Knit 18 rows in the skirt colour. When you finish the 18 rows, leave a long tail on the skirt colour again and switch back to the scrap yarn.

Knit five rows in the scrap yarn. When you finish, cut a short tail and continue knitting until the work falls off the needles. Pull the work out of the machine and gently stretch out the stitches. You should now have two pieces knit and ready to assemble: the main piece for the doll and the skirt.

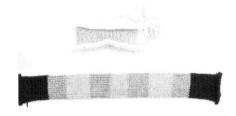

Step 3:

Assembling the doll. Begin by turning the work inside out. You'll have lots of yarn tails from all the colour changes. Secure each colour change tails with a few good knots and trim the tails. As you work, check the outside of the piece to ensure that you're pulling tight enough that the stitches are close together but not so tight that the stitches get bunched up. Then, turn the piece on the right side out.

Use a yarn tail from one of the sides, which will be the hair colour. To cinch the top of the doll's hair together, gently pull the tail and roll the work inside as you cinch. Thread the tail onto a darning needle and secure it with a few knots, capturing stitches from several sides of the closure.

Next, push the closure inside the work to meet the other hair colour section. It can be a little awkward to figure out the first time you make a doll but wiggle it around, and you'll get it.

When the two sides are together, thread the tail from the bottom inside the piece to exit at the top of the doll. When you have both tails together, use the exterior tail to cinch the top of the doll again, making sure to roll the work inside as you cinch.

After both sides are cinched, tie a few good knots between the tail yarns, weave in the tails to the centre of the work, leaving the yarn tail between the two layers, and trim the ends. Next, grab your stuffing and gently add it to the doll.

Don't overstuff the doll, or it will stretch out the stitches. Add it slowly, a bit at a time, pushing it around so it's evenly placed. Twist the doll in the areas you'll be cinching later to ensure enough stuffing in each area.

After you finish stuffing the doll, thread a length of yarn in the shoe colour onto a darning needle and thread it through the first half of each stitch around the bottom until the end of the row. Then, pull the yarn to close the feet. Tie the two yarn tails together tightly and weave in the ends to the inside of the work.

It's really easy to hide the ends when making a doll. Just thread them into the centre of the work, pull the thread, trim it, and then wiggle the work to pull the tail into the body's centre. The doll is assembled.

Step 4:

Adding the facial and body features. Identify which will be the front and which will be the back of your doll. Typically, place the side with the yarn changes on the back of the doll since some stitches will likely look a little off.

First, add the definition between the head and the body. Grab a length of yarn in the face yarn and begin at the back of the doll. Thread the yarn through the first half of each stitch and continue until the end of the row.

Then, pull the yarn as tight as you can without breaking it and tie a knot on the back of the doll. Bring the yarn once around the outside and pull it as tightly as possible. Secure it with a couple of good knots on the back, then weave in and trim the ends. Next, repeat the same process about a third from the top to create the bun.

Next, we'll shape the legs. Grab a length of yarn in the shoe colour yarn and tie a quick knot on the interior bar to secure the yarn in the back. Sew back and forth, starting from the centre bottom until you reach the top of the shoes.

Thread the yarn to the back, secure it with a knot, and weave in the yarn tail to the centre. When you reach the legs, switch to the leg yarn colour and repeat the same process, sewing up in a line to create the legs. Then, secure the yarn with a quick knot in the back and weave in the ends.

Next, create the arms. Use the same process with the shirt collar to sew back and forth on the side to create the arm segments on both sides.

Next, add the ballet slipper straps. Grab the shoe yarn collar and start by securing the yarn in the back of the doll with a knot on an interior bar, then thread it through to the front centre. Wrap the yarn around the leg and thread the needle under a bar on the side of the leg a little further to the back. Then thread back to the area we started, but make sure to go through a different stitch. Repeat the same process on the other leg and thread it back through the same area to the back. Thread the needle up a few stitches and do the opposite wrapping, going from the top to the bottom, securing the yarn through an interior stitch on the side of the doll to keep it in place. Repeat on the other leg, then thread the needle to the back, secure it with a knot, and weave in the ends.

Next, add the facial features. Keep the facial features super simple in dolls. Use a black embroidery thread to create two eyes. When done, secure the embroidery thread in the back with a knot and weave in the ends. Repeat the same process with the pink yarn to create a mouth. The ballerina is starting to come together.

Step 5:

Seam the skirt. Assembling the skirt is essentially the same process as making a scrunchie. Turn the work inside out with the V-shaped stitches on the inside and the bumpy stitches on the outside.

Wrap a hair elastic around the middle, line up the top row of main colour stitches, and use a crochet hook to go through the first stitch on the bottom. Then, pull through the stitch above it.

Next, pull through the next stitch on the top to the left, then the next stitch on the bottom. Continue in that pattern, pulling through loops from the top and then the bottom, and repeat until the end of the circle. When you reach the end, capture all the last couple of stitches, then tie a quick knot between the two yarn tails.

Step 6:

Removing the scrap yarn. Your skirt will still have the scrap yarn from when we cast on and cast off. Begin to pull the yarn to remove it; one side will likely pull off easily. For the other side, identify the yarn thread that runs through the top stitches. Remove it a few stitches until the end of the row.

Once the length is removed, the rest of the yarn should pull off easily. When you're done, secure the yarn tails with a few good knots and weave in the ends. Add a knitting tag to the back of the skirt.

Step 7:

Adding the skirt. This step is very easy since we used hair elastic; the skirt will be stretchy, and you can place it onto the doll. If you plan to make a selection of skirts for your doll, like a dress-up doll, leave the skirt unattached. If you're only using one skirt, add a few stitches to secure the skirt to the doll, so it can't be moved out of place.

Step 8:

Knitting a bow. Create a bow for the doll in so many ways: rochet the bow, sew a fabric, use a store-bought bow, or you could even make it with a 22-needle machine.

Use a pair of US size 7 needles; using circulars, but straight needles are fine, too. Cast on 10 stitches using the long-tail cast-on method. Then, work in double stockinette stitch for two and a half inches.

To knit a double stockinette, it's a simple repeat: knit one stitch, bring the yarn to the front, slip the next stitch, and then bring the yarn to the back; repeat until the end of the row. For every row, when you get to two and a half inches, bind off in the same pattern. Next, take a length of yarn and wrap it around the middle of the bow over and over until it's cinched, leaving two yarn tails in the back.

Secure the yarn tails with a knot on the back of the bow. If you want your bow to be removable, tie the bow in the same way you would tie shoes. But if you'd like the bow to stay attached to your doll, stitch right into it to secure it with a needle.

The ballerina is done.

Chapter Nine

DIY Products

<u>DIY Headband</u>: A simple pattern for knitting a headband using a circular machine.

Loom Knit Holiday Bag: A more advanced pattern for creating a stylish bag using a circular knitting machine. Addi Boho Towel Ring: A unique pattern for knitting a decorative towel ring that adds a touch of elegance to any bathroom.

Maci Beanie: A cosy beanie pattern suitable for beginners, perfect for keeping hands warm during colder months

.

Colourful Twist Headband: A fun and colourful headband pattern that adds colour to any outfit.

DIY Rainbow Wall Hanging: A visually appealing wall-hanging pattern that adds a touch of creativity to any room.

Brioche Stitch

Advantages of DIY Headbands

DIY headbands offer several advantages, making them popular for individuals looking to create accessories. Some of the key advantages include:

Customization: One of the primary benefits of DIY headbands is the ability to customize them according to personal preferences. Individuals can choose their preferred colours, patterns, and materials, allowing for a unique and personalized accessory.

Cost-Effective: Creating headbands at home can be a cost-effective alternative to purchasing them from stores. Individuals can save money using readily available materials or repurposing existing items while achieving stylish headbands.

Creativity and Self-Expression: DIY headbands provide an avenue for creativity and self-expression. Individuals can experiment with different designs, embellishments, and techniques, allowing them to showcase their unique style and personality through their accessories.

Sustainability: Making headbands at home aligns with sustainable practices by reducing the reliance on mass-produced accessories. Individuals can contribute to environmental conservation efforts by using recycled or eco-friendly materials.

Therapeutic and Relaxing: Engaging in DIY headband projects can be relaxing. It offers a creative outlet that can help reduce stress and anxiety while providing a sense of accomplishment upon completing the project.

Disadvantages of DIY Headbands

While DIY headbands offer numerous advantages, there are also some potential disadvantages to consider:

Time-Consuming: Creating DIY headbands may require a significant time investment, especially for individuals new to crafting or sewing. Selecting materials, designing, and assembling the headbands can be time-consuming.

Skill and Expertise Required: Certain DIY headband designs may necessitate specific crafting skills or expertise in sewing, knitting, or other techniques. Individuals without experience in these areas may face challenges in achieving the desired results.

Quality Variability: The quality of DIY headbands may vary based on individual crafting abilities and the materials used. Sometimes, homemade headbands may not match the durability and finish of professionally manufactured ones.

Limited Resources: Access to a wide range of materials and tools may be limited for some individuals, impacting their ability to create diverse or intricate headband designs.

Initial Investment: While DIY headbands can be cost-effective in the long run, initial investment may be required to purchase crafting supplies and tools, which could deter some individuals from pursuing this hobby.

Variations of the Brioche Stitch: The brioche stitch can be knitted in various ways, such as the classic brioche stitch, the two-colour brioche stitch, and the cable brioche stitch.

How the Brioche Stitch is Knitted: The brioche stitch is a technique that involves working with two strands of yarn at once, creating a soft and warm fabric. It is a more advanced stitch but can be mastered with practice.

Teardrop Stitch

Interweave Knits: Interweave Knits is a magazine and online resource that offers patterns, techniques, and inspiration for knitters of all skill levels. It was used to find advanced circular knitting machine patterns, such as the loom knit holiday bag and the DIY rainbow wall hanging.

Loom Knit Holiday Bag

This is a type of bag made out of knitting. Here are some steps to consider to neat a bag of this kind.

Assemble the supplies: a round loom (size will vary depending on the size desired for a bag), holiday-coloured yarn, loom hook, yarn needle, scissors, and any embellishments you wish to add.

Select Stitch: Choose a stitch design that works well for your bag. Beginners can start with simple knit or purl stitches, but you can experiment with more intricate ones for more texture. To begin knitting, cast a few stitches onto the loom. Knit rows in the pattern of your choice until the bag reaches the desired height. Do not forget to allow sufficient yarn for the drawstring closure at the top of the bag.

Shape the Bag: Work in equal amounts of stitches around the last few rows to make a flat bottom for the bag. The bag will take on a square or rectangular shape as a result.

Bind Off: Join your stitches to create your bag's desired height and shape. This will hold the bag's top and prepare it for finishing. Last touches: trim extra yarn and weave in any loose ends. Your holiday bag can be adorned with buttons, beads, or ribbons if you'd like.

Make a drawstring: Crochet or knit a drawstring using the same yarn as your bag or contrasting colour. A yarn needle should be used to thread it through the top of your bag. Final Adjustments: Pull the drawstring tight to seal the bag's top. To hold the drawstring in place, tie knots at both ends.

Enjoy Your Bag: Now that your loom-knit holiday bag is ready to use, fill it with festive treats, gifts, or other goodies to help spread the holiday spirit. Try it: Don't be hesitant to try out new things.

Addi Boho Towel Ring

To make an Addi Boho Towel Ring, you'll need a towel ring, yarn in the colours of your choice, a crochet hook, and an Addi Express Knitting Machine.

How to Make It: Assemble your Addi Express Knitting Machine following the manufacturer's instructions to set it up. Make that a stable surface where it is firmly attached.

Pick Yarn: Choose your yarn in the colours you want. Though you can choose colours and yarn types, boho-style designs typically feature earthy tones and natural fibres.

Start Knitting: Using the Addi Express, begin knitting a tube using the colours of yarn you have selected. Work with a basic stockinette stitch or try other patterns to keep things simple.

Incorporate Texture: If you want your knitting to have a bohemian vibe, add some texture. This can be achieved by switching up the kinds of yarn (e.g., G. adding fringe or adding tiny knitted or crocheted embellishments., using a thick-and-thin yarn. To create a loop, bind off your stitches after knitting a tube long enough to fit around your towel ring. To sew the ends together, leave a tail of yarn.

Attach Towel Ring: Place the towel ring close to one end of the knitted tube and thread it through. Make sure the ring is firmly and centrally placed.

Join Ends: Use the knitted tube's ends to create a loop by sewing them with a crochet hook and the leftover yarn tail. Ensure that the seam is neat and safe.

Lasting Details: Cut off any extra yarn and tidy up Check for excess yarn; this is the final stage of checking the details.

Maci Beanie

Knitting a Maci beanie involves creating a cosy and stylish hat using specific techniques and patterns. The Maci beanie is known for its textured stitches, often featuring cables or other intricate designs. To knit a Maci beanie, follow a pattern that outlines the required stitches, yarn type, and needle size. Additionally, understanding basic knitting techniques such as casting on, knitting, purling, and decreasing stitches is essential for successfully creating a Maci beanie.

To begin knitting a Maci beanie, you will need to gather the necessary materials, including yarn in the colour of your choice, appropriately sized knitting needles, a cable needle if the pattern includes cables, and a tapestry needle for finishing. It's important to select a yarn that complements the desired texture and warmth of the beanie. Once your materials are ready, you can start casting on the required number of stitches as specified in the pattern.

Following the pattern instructions, you will knit the beanie's body using the designated stitch pattern. Depending on the chosen design, this may involve working in rounds or rows. If the pattern includes cables, you will use a cable needle to cross stitches and create a distinctive cable motif. As you progress through the pattern, you will systematically shape the beanie crown by decreasing stitches until only a few remain.

You will need yarn in the desired colour, scissors, knitting needles matching the yarn weight, and a tapestry needle to knit a Maci Beanie. To get you started, here's a basic pattern:

Gauge Swatch: To find your stitches per inch, start by knitting a gauge swatch. This will guarantee that the beanie you make fits well.

 Cast On: After figuring out your gauge, cast on the number of stitches needed to achieve your desired size. Depending on your gauge and preferred fit, you may begin with a standard adult-size beanie with 80–100 stitches.

Ribbing: For stretchiness, start with a ribbed brim. For a timeless style, use a k1, p1 ribbing pattern. Knit to desired brim length or about 1-2 inches in ribbing.

Body: For the beanie's body, change from ribbing to stockinette stitch (knit all stitches on right side rows, purl all stitches on wrong side rows). Knit the hat until it reaches your desired length or about 7-8 inches from the cast-on edge.

Crown Decreases: You will need to decrease stitches to shape the beanie's crown gradually. A simple decrease pattern follows Row 1: Knit 6, knit 2 together, and repeat to the end of the row. Row 2: Work every stitch. Continue these two rows, decreasing by one stitch every other row, until you have about 8–12 stitches remaining.

Closing: Cut the yarn, making sure to leave a long tail. To close the beanie's crown, thread the tail onto a tapestry needle and pull tightly through the remaining stitches.

Colorful twist headband.
A colourful twist headband is a stylish and versatile accessory that adds colour and flair to any outfit. These headbands are typically made from a stretchy fabric and feature a twisted design at the front, creating an eye-catching and fashionable look. They come in various colours and patterns, making them suitable for casual outings and formal events.

Features of Colorful Twist Headbands
Colourful twist headbands are known for their unique design and practicality. The twisted front detail adds visual interest and dimension to the headband, making

it stand out as a fashion statement. The stretchy nature of the fabric ensures a comfortable and secure fit for different head sizes, making them suitable for adults and children. The available colours and patterns allow individuals to express their style and coordinate the headband with different outfits.

Versatility and Styling Options

One of the key advantages of colourful twist headbands is their versatility. They can be worn with various hairstyles, including loose hair, ponytails, or buns, making them suitable for different hair lengths and textures. Whether it's a casual day out, a workout session, or a special occasion, these headbands can complement different looks and add a playful touch to any ensemble. Furthermore, they are often lightweight and easy to pack, making them convenient for travel or on-the-go styling.

Where to Find Colorful Twist Headbands

Colourful twist headbands can be found in various retail outlets, including fashion accessory stores, department stores, online marketplaces, and speciality boutiques. Many brands offer these headbands in assorted colour palettes and designs, allowing customers to choose options that align with their preferences.

DIY Rainbow Wall Hanging

Gather materials: You will need the following items:

Fabric or felt in various rainbow colours (red, orange, yellow, green, blue, and purple)

Scissors

Sewing machine or hot glue gun

Thread or glue sticks that match the fabric colors

A long string or ribbon for hanging

A ruler or measuring tape

Pins or fabric weights

Measure and cut fabric pieces: a. Determine the size of the rainbow wall hanging you want to create. b. Measure and cut the fabric or felt into rectangular or square shapes. The size of each piece can vary, but ensure they are consistent within each colour of the rainbow.

Create a rainbow pattern: Arrange the fabric pieces in a rainbow order (red, orange, yellow, green, blue, and purple). b. Pin or weigh down the fabric pieces to keep them in place while you work on the next step.

Sew or glue the fabric pieces together: a. If using a sewing machine, sew the fabric pieces together in a straight line along one of the shorter edges, starting with red and ending with purple. b. If using a hot glue gun, apply a glue line along one of the shorter edges of each fabric piece and press them together, ensuring the colours match the rainbow order. Allow the glue to dry completely.

Attach the hanging string or ribbon: Measure and cut a long string or ribbon long enough to hang the rainbow wall on your desired wall. b. Fold the string or ribbon in half to create a loop. c. Sew or glue the loop to the top of the rainbow, ensuring it is secure and centred.

Hang the rainbow wall hanging: Locate the appropriate spot where you want to hang the rainbow. b. Use a nail or adhesive hook to secure the string or ribbon loop to the wall. c. Adjust the rainbow's position to ensure it is straight and centred.

Brioche Stitch

Brioche stitch is a knitting technique that creates a lofty, reversible fabric with a unique texture. Its distinctive ribbed appearance characterizes it and is often used to create warm and cosy garments such as scarves, hats, and sweaters. The stitch is achieved by working yarn over and slipping stitches together, creating a squishy, cushioned fabric.

How to Knit Brioche Stitch

To knit the brioche stitch, you must use a special technique that involves working with two colours of yarn and slipping stitches. The basic steps for knitting brioche stitch include casting on an even number of stitches, setting up the first row with a setup row, and then alternating between knit and purl stitches while slipping certain stitches with yarn overs to create the characteristic brioche texture.

Applications of Brioche Stitch

Brioche stitch is commonly used to create knitted items such as scarves, cowls, shawls, and sweaters. Its reversible nature makes it ideal for projects where both sides of the fabric are visible. Brioche stitch can be combined with other knitting techniques to create intricate patterns and designs.

Benefits of Brioche Stitch

One of the main benefits of brioche stitch is its warmth and squishiness due to the double-layered fabric it creates. This makes it particularly suitable for cold-weather accessories and garments. Additionally, the reversible nature of brioche stitch adds versatility to knitted pieces, allowing for different looks on each side.

Challenges of Knitting Brioche Stitch

While brioche stitch produces beautiful results, it can be more complex than traditional knitting techniques, especially for beginners. Keeping track of the different yarn-overs and slipped stitches may require extra attention and concentration. However, with practice, knitters can master this unique stitch and enjoy the stunning textures it produces.

Variations of the Brioche Stitch

The brioche stitch is a beautiful and versatile knitting technique that creates a lofty, reversible fabric with a unique texture. The brioche stitch has several variations, each offering its distinct look and feel. These variations can involve different combinations of knit, purl, and yarn-over stitches and working with multiple colours. Here are some common variations of the brioche stitch:

Basic Brioche Stitch: The basic brioche stitch involves working a combination of a slipped stitch yarn over (sl1yo) and a brioche knit (brk) or brioche purl (brp) stitch. This creates a ribbed fabric with a distinctive texture.

Two-Color Brioche Stitch: In two-color brioche, two contrasting yarns create a stunning reversible fabric with a deeply textured appearance. This variation often involves working with two colours in a row and using specific techniques to create intricate colour patterns.

Fisherman's Rib: While not technically a brioche stitch, fisherman's rib is often considered a variation due to its similarities. This technique creates a plush, stretchy fabric that resembles brioche but is achieved through different methods, such as knitting into the row below.

Syncopated Brioche: Syncopated brioche introduces additional complexity by alternating the placement of the slipped stitches and yarn-overs, resulting in an interplay of textures and colours that can be visually striking.

Honeycomb Brioche: This variation creates a honeycomb-like texture by combining brioche stitches with slipped stitches worked over multiple rows. The result is a deeply textured fabric that adds visual interest to any project.

Garter Stitch Brioche: Garter stitch brioche combines garter stitch with the brioche technique to produce a squishy, reversible fabric showcasing knit and purl textures.

Tuck Stitch Brioche: Tuck stitch brioche incorporates tucking stitches behind others to create raised motifs within the fabric. This variation adds dimension and visual appeal to brioche knitting projects.

How the Brioche Stitch is Knitted

The brioche stitch is a beautiful and unique knitting technique that creates a lofty, reversible fabric with a lovely texture. It is often used to create scarves, shawls, and other garments. To knit the brioche stitch, you will need to follow these steps:

Step 1: Cast On Begin by casting on an even number of stitches using your preferred method. The brioche stitch requires an even number of stitches to work properly.

Step 2: Setup Row For the setup row, knit one stitch, yarn over, and slip 1 across the entire row. This will create the foundation for the brioche stitch pattern.

Step 3: First Pass On the first pass of the brioche stitch pattern, you will work with two different yarns. Hold one yarn in your left hand and the other in your right. Begin by knitting the next stitch with its accompanying yarn from the setup row. Then, yarn over slip 1 across the row.

Step 4: Second Pass: you will work with just one yarn for the second pass. Slip the first stitch purlwise, yarn over, and slip 1 across the row.

Step 5: Repeat. Continue alternating between the first and second passes to create the brioche stitch pattern. The result will be a plush, reversible fabric with a distinctive ribbed texture.

Step 6: Bind Off When you have reached your desired length, bind off your stitches using a stretchy bind-off method to maintain the elasticity of the brioche stitch.

Following these steps, you can create a beautifully textured fabric using the brioche stitch technique.

Teardrop Stitch

The teardrop stitch is a decorative embroidery stitch that resembles a teardrop shape. It is commonly used in hand embroidery to create intricate and delicate designs on fabric. The stitch is formed by creating a series of small straight stitches that converge at a central point, forming the teardrop shape. This stitch can create floral motifs, leaves, and other organic shapes in embroidery projects.

How to Create the Teardrop Stitch

To create the teardrop stitch, follow these steps:
Bring the needle up through the fabric at the starting point of the teardrop shape.
Make a small straight stitch in the desired direction of the teardrop, ensuring that the length matches the desired length of the teardrop.
Bring the

Here's how to do the teardrop stitch:
Start by bringing your needle up through the fabric at the starting point of your teardrop shape.
Insert the needle back into the fabric slightly to the side of the starting point, forming the narrow end of the teardrop.

Bring the needle up again at a point further along the teardrop shape, forming the wider end of the teardrop. Insert the needle back into the fabric at the same point where you started the wide end of the teardrop, but slightly to the side, creating a curve.

Continue this process, alternating sides as you move along the teardrop shape until you reach the desired length.

To finish the stitch, bring the needle to the back of the fabric and secure the thread.

Remember to keep your stitches consistent in length and spacing for a neat and uniform appearance. Practice on a scrap fabric until you feel comfortable with the technique.

Abbreviations in Knitting

In knitting, abbreviations are commonly used to make patterns more concise and easier to read. These abbreviations represent specific stitches, techniques, or instructions. Understanding these abbreviations is essential for following knitting patterns accurately.

Here are some common knitting abbreviations and their meanings:

K: Knit

P: Purl

YO: Yarn over

SSK: Slip, slip, knit

K2tog: Knit two together

P2tog: Purl two together

PM: Place marker

SM: Slip marker

RS: Right side

WS: Wrong side

These are just a few examples of the many knitting abbreviations used in patterns. Each pattern may have its unique set of abbreviations, so it's important to refer to the key or legend provided in the pattern to understand the specific abbreviations used.

Instructions in Knitting

Knitting instructions can vary widely depending on the pattern and the desired outcome. However, some common instructions appear frequently in knitting patterns. These instructions dictate how to perform specific stitches or techniques to create the desired fabric. Some common knitting instructions include:

Cast on: This is the foundation of any knitting project, where stitches are added to the needle before beginning the main pattern.

Knit: This basic stitch creates a smooth fabric and is often abbreviated as "K" in patterns.

Purl: The purl stitch creates a bumpy texture on the fabric and is often abbreviated as "P" in patterns.

Yarn over (YO): This technique adds an extra stitch and creates small eyelets in the fabric.

Increase: There are various methods for increasing stitches, such as yarn overs or knitting into the front and back of a stitch.

Decrease: Similarly, there are different ways to decrease stitches, including knitting two together (K2tog) and slip, slip, knit (SSK).

Bind off (or cast off): This is the process of finishing the edge of the knitted piece and securing the stitches so they don't unravel.

Following these instructions carefully is crucial for achieving the intended design of a knitted item.

www.ingramcontent.com/pod-product-compliance
Ingram Content Group UK Ltd.
Pitfield, Milton Keynes, MK11 3LW, UK
UKHW021417170225
4625UKWH00036B/946